Published by Sequoia Kids Media,
an imprint of Sequoia Publishing & Media, LLC

Sequoia Publishing & Media, LLC,
a division of Phoenix International Publications, Inc.

8501 West Higgins Road, Chicago, Illinois 60631
34 Seymour Street, London W1H 7JE
Heimhuder Straße 81, 20148 Hamburg

© 2023 Sequoia Publishing & Media, LLC

Customer Service: cs@sequoiakidsbooks.com

Sequoia Kids Media and associated logo are trademarks and/
or registered trademarks of Sequoia Publishing & Media, LLC.

Active Minds is a registered trademark of Phoenix International
Publications, Inc., and is used with permission.

All rights reserved. This publication may not be reproduced in whole
or in part by any means without permission from the copyright owners.
Permission is never granted for commercial purposes.

www.SequoiaKidsMedia.com

ISBN 978-1-64996-169-3

CHECK OUT THE END OF SURF'S UP FOR SEA OTTERS! FOR DEFINITIONS TO BOLDED WORDS.

SURF'S UP FOR SEA OTTERS!

Written by Valerie J. Weber
Illustrated by Rachel Sanson

Owen C. Otter sleeps on his back, rocked by the ocean. His mother holds his hand to keep him close. His friends sleep nearby. The **kelp** bed stops them from floating away.

At dawn, his friend Finn gives him a nudge.

Wake up, Owen! It's time!

Owen untangles himself from the kelp. His dream is about to come true! Finn is going to teach him how to **body surf**!

"I thought you were going to pick **sea urchins** out of the kelp today."

"Can I do it when I get back?"

Owen has been working on becoming a better swimmer. He does exercises every day. His tail and back feet are strong!

Mom says Owen can go if he takes his friends, too.

Owen heard his cousins, the **river otters**, had started body surfing. He has thought about surfing in the ocean ever since.

Owen watches the waves. They look big. Owen gulps.

Finn surfs through the water. He makes it easy.

Owen **paddles** in place. Dolphins are good at **skimming** on top of the waves. Otters are better at diving *under* the waves. He paddles in place some more.

Owen holds his breath and closes his ears.
He paddles as fast as he can.

Whoops! Owen tumbles under a wave.

Owen tries again. And again. He almost has it—but then he wipes out. Maybe sea otters aren't meant to surf after all.

Owen decides he'll try again another day. He calls to his friends to go home. He turns—and sees the most perfect wave. And then...

Thanks to their teamwork, the otters master surfing in no time. Finally, after a long, fun day, it's time to go home.

Owen and his friends swim, twirl, and twist their way home together, the otter way.

New Words from Surf's Up for Sea Otters!

 **body surf (BAH-dee SURF):** floating on the highest part of a wave without using a board. Dolphins have long, streamlined bodies that are perfect for body surfing.

 **river otter (RIV-uhr OTT-uhr):** a type of otter that lives near lakes and rivers. River otters are much smaller than sea otters.

 **kelp (KELP):** a type of seaweed. Sea otters live in kelp forests. Kelp that grows quickly underwater makes up kelp forests.

 **sea urchin (SEE UHR-chin):** a spiny animal that lives in the ocean. Sea urchins live in kelp forests. They eat a lot, including a lot of kelp. Too many sea urchins can destroy a kelp forest.

 **paddle (pad-DUHL):** to swim by using arms and legs to move. Sea otters paddle their back legs to swim.

 **skimming (SKIM-ing):** to move through water without touching the bottom. Dolphins have smooth skin and pointed noses that help them skim through the water.

NOW FLIP THE BOOK TO LEARN FUN FACTS ABOUT OTTERS!

Fun Fact

River otters swim on their stomachs. They keep most of their bodies underwater. They also climb out of the water and rest on riverbanks. Sea otters like to swim on their backs. They mostly live in the water.

"Moms make the best life jackets!"

Sea otters can hold their breath underwater for five minutes. Most humans can't hold their breath for more than a minute.

Sea otters are the only otters born in the water. They don't learn to swim until they are two months old. They must float with their mothers or on top of the water until then.

NOW FLIP THE BOOK TO READ A STORY ABOUT A SEA OTTER WHO LEARNS TO BODY SURF!

Swimming is my super power!

Sea otters get the water they need from the food they eat. They can even safely drink salty sea water if they're really feeling thirsty.

Sea otters are sleek and streamlined. They tumble, somersault, spin, and race through the water. Webbed feet help them swim at around 0.9 miles (1.5 kilometers) per hour on the ocean's surface. Their top speed underwater is 5.6 miles (9 km) per hour. To keep the water out of their bodies, they close their nostrils and ears.

Fun Fact

River otters do not have pockets. They must keep their tools on land and bring their food to them.

Otters in captivity can be trained to raise their paws. This makes it easy to show humans what's in their pockets.

I have a secret...pocket!

Sea otters have a secret! Below each arm is a pocket-like flap of loose skin. It is baggy enough to hold a tennis ball. But what are the pockets used for? A pocket might hold a tool, like a favorite rock for smashing shells. Or it could keep a tasty treat, like some clams or a fish, to eat later.

I can keep ten mussels in my pocket.

Baby otters are called pups. They learn to use tools from their mothers. Kelp is a tool, too. Mother sea otters wrap their babies tightly in kelp.

Sea otter moms usually only have one pup at a time.

Fun Fact

Thanks to their fluffy fur, baby otters float. But they can't swim anywhere. Wrapping babies in kelp keeps them from floating away while their mothers hunt.

We're clever critters!

Much of what sea otters eat is curled up tightly inside shells. But it's not a problem for sea otters. They are one of the few ocean mammals that use tools. Smashing a rock on a shell to crack it open is an easy way to find a meal.

Some otters even have favorite tools. Determined otters use bottles, driftwood, or cans to crush shells. Others smash shells on the sides of boats.

By eating sea urchins, sea otters help their kelp forest homes stay healthy. Kelp forests remove extra carbon dioxide from the atmosphere. Carbon dioxide is a greenhouse gas that holds heat. Too much of this gas makes Earth too warm. By helping kelp forests stay healthy, otters also help our planet!

Sea otters can eat up to one-fourth of their weight each day. Imagine how much food that would be for you!

Sea urchin with a kelp salad on the side, please.

So, what's for lunch?

Otters feed on fish and shellfish. Shellfish are animals with a protective shell, like crayfish, crabs, oysters, and clams. River otters also eat frogs, bird eggs, and reptiles. An important food for sea otters are sea urchins. The urchins eat a lot of kelp. This destroys the kelp forests where many animals, including sea otters, live.

Fun Fact

River otters also eat plants. Sometimes they even hunt small animals, like rabbits and birds.

Keeping clean is important to otters. They can spend nearly half their time grooming each other. Clean fur is warm fur. Mother otters groom their babies for the first three months of their lives. They also blow air into the babies' fur.

My fluffy fur helps me float!

Otters are fur-tastic!

Most marine animals have a thick layer of fat called blubber. It helps them stay warm in cold oceans. But otters don't have blubber. Instead, they have thick fur. Otter fur is so thick that water can't get in. Sea otters have thicker fur than any other mammal—between 500,000 and 1 million hairs per square inch! Humans only have 800 to 1,290 hairs per square inch. Can you imagine what otter fur feels like?

Where in the world do otters live?

Fun Fact

Giant otters live in South America. They usually eat fish. But they also hunt anacondas, piranhas, and alligators called caimans.

sea otter

river otter

sea otter

MAP KEY
- WHERE RIVER OTTERS LIVE
- WHERE SEA OTTERS LIVE